CW01163326

WHAT ABOUT THANKSGIVING

WRITTEN BY TOMMY WATKINS

Halloween had passed, and Thanksgiving was coming.

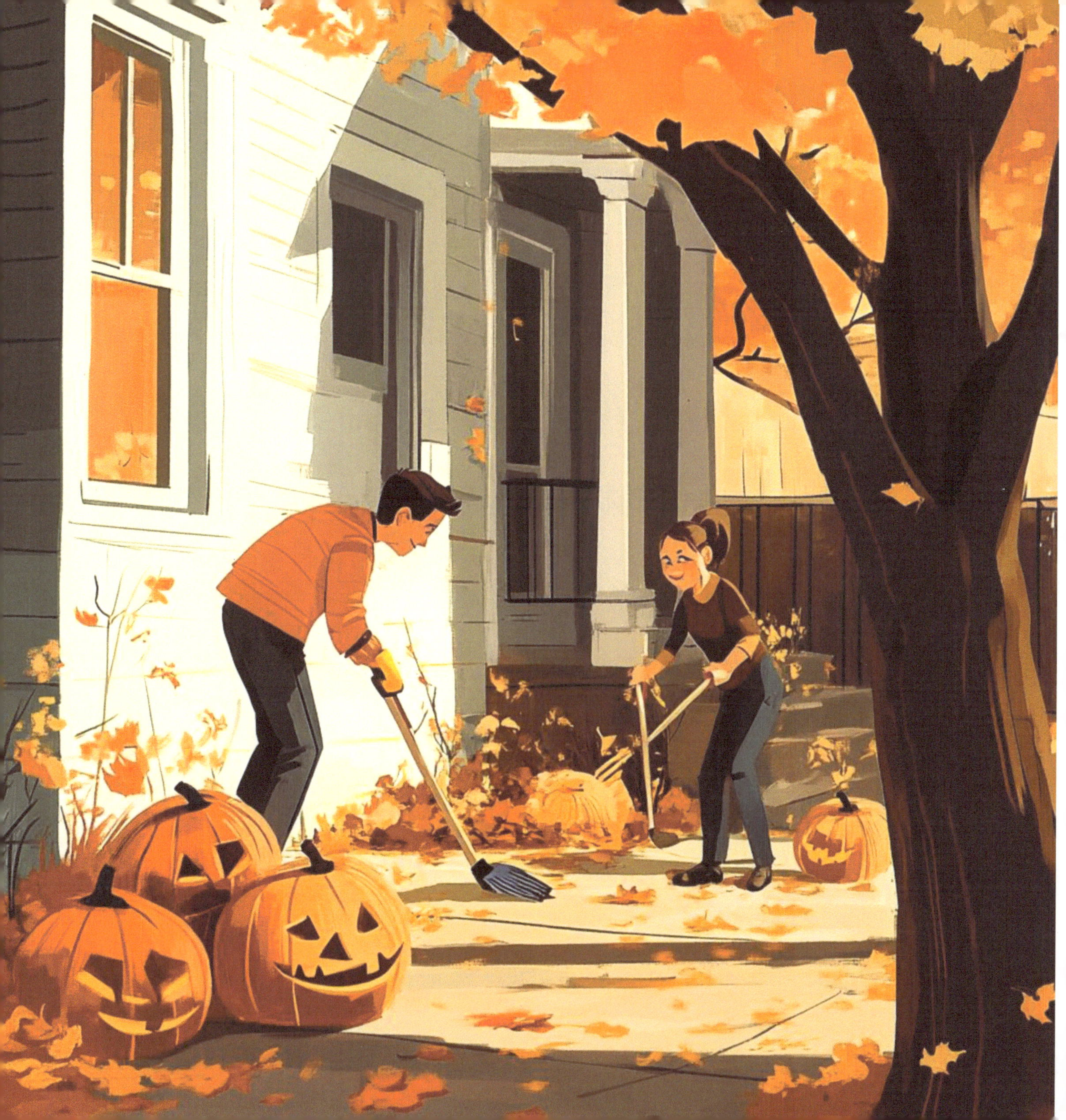

Everyone in the town started
putting up their Christmas lights.
Even in the local store,
Christmas promotions were out.

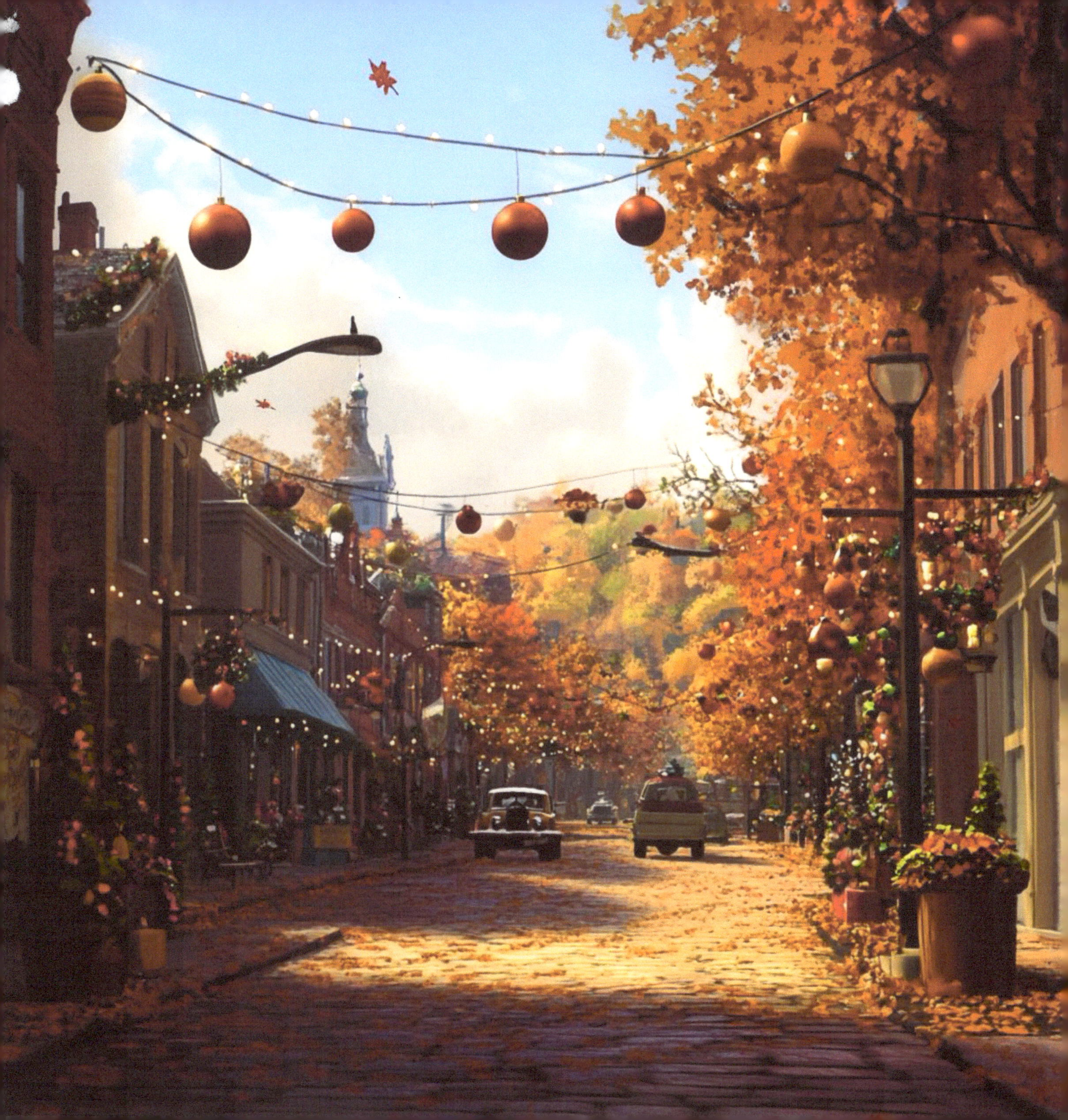

Abby was walking through her town seeing this madness.

What about Thanksgiving?

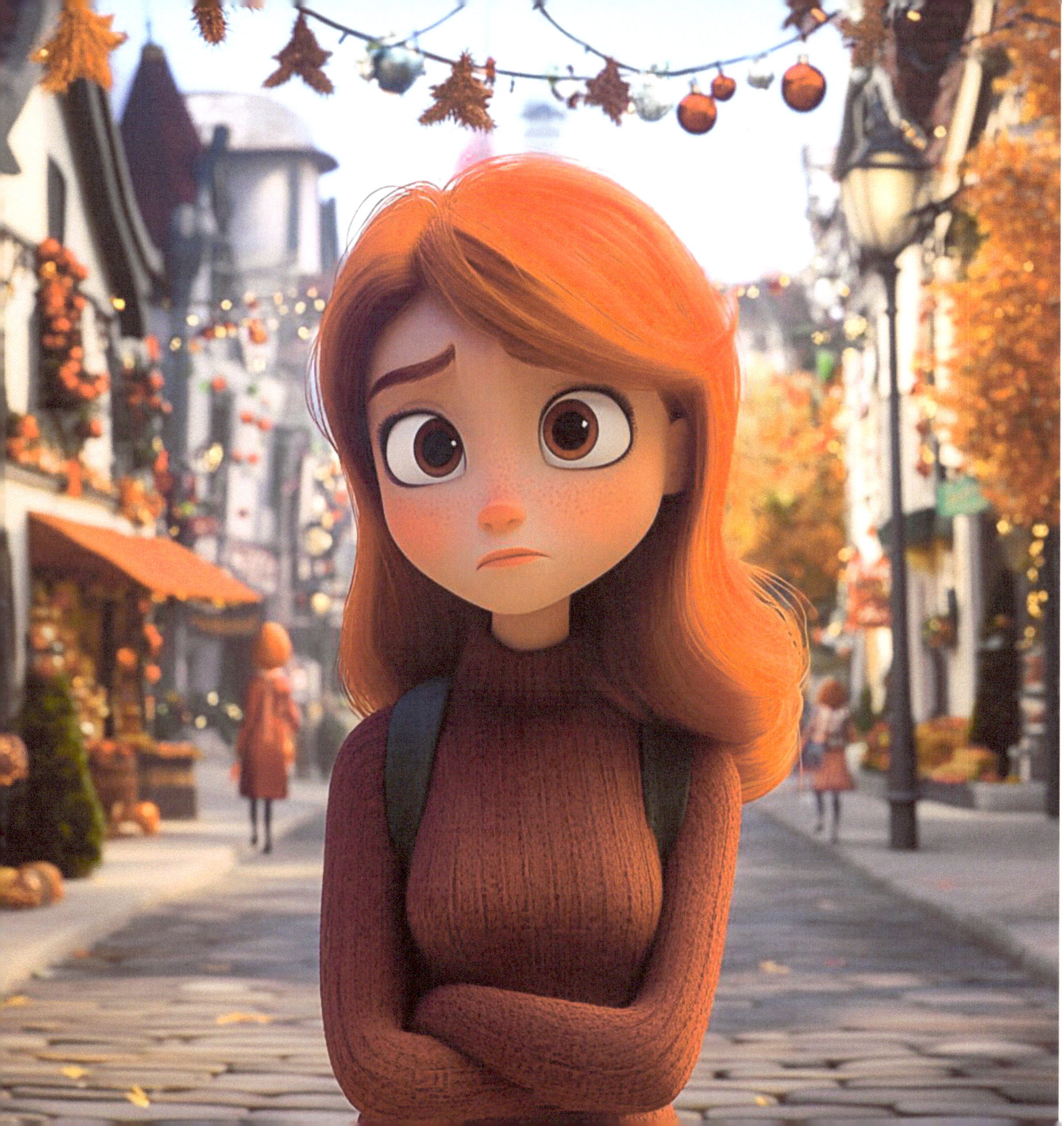

The day would be filled
with platters of delicious food.

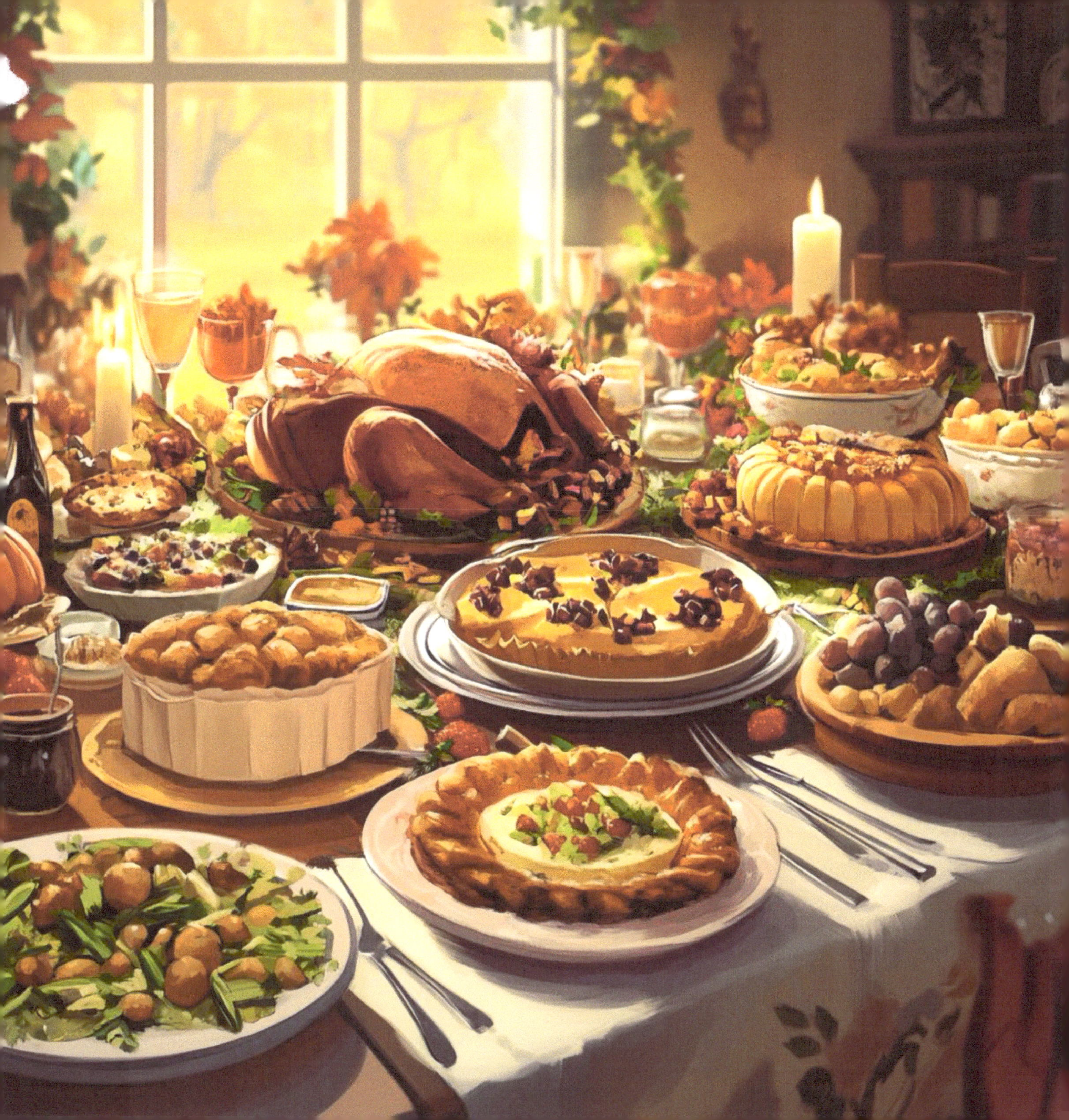

Families gathering together at the dinner table.

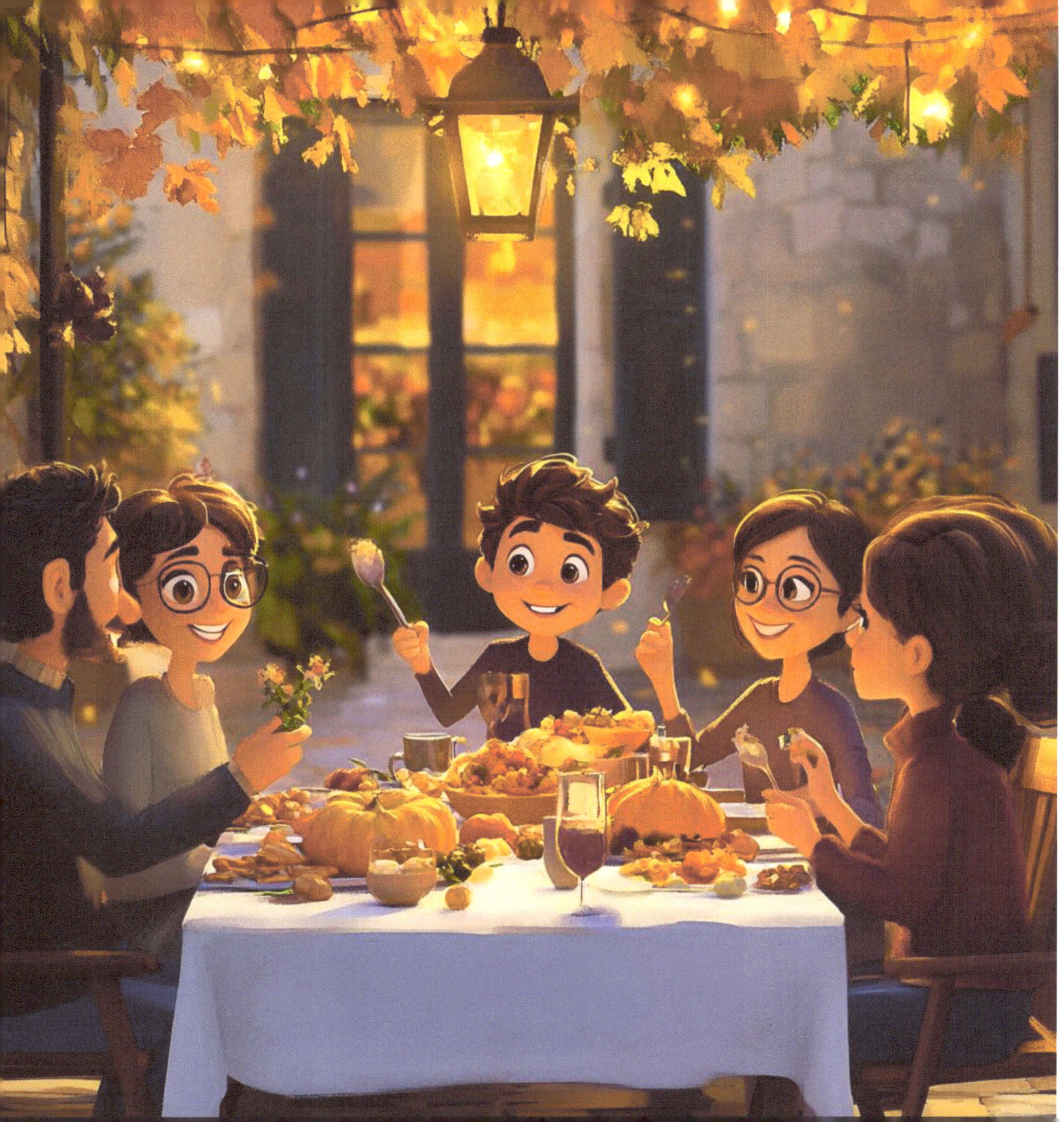

Thanksgiving would be complete
with a football game
playing on the television.

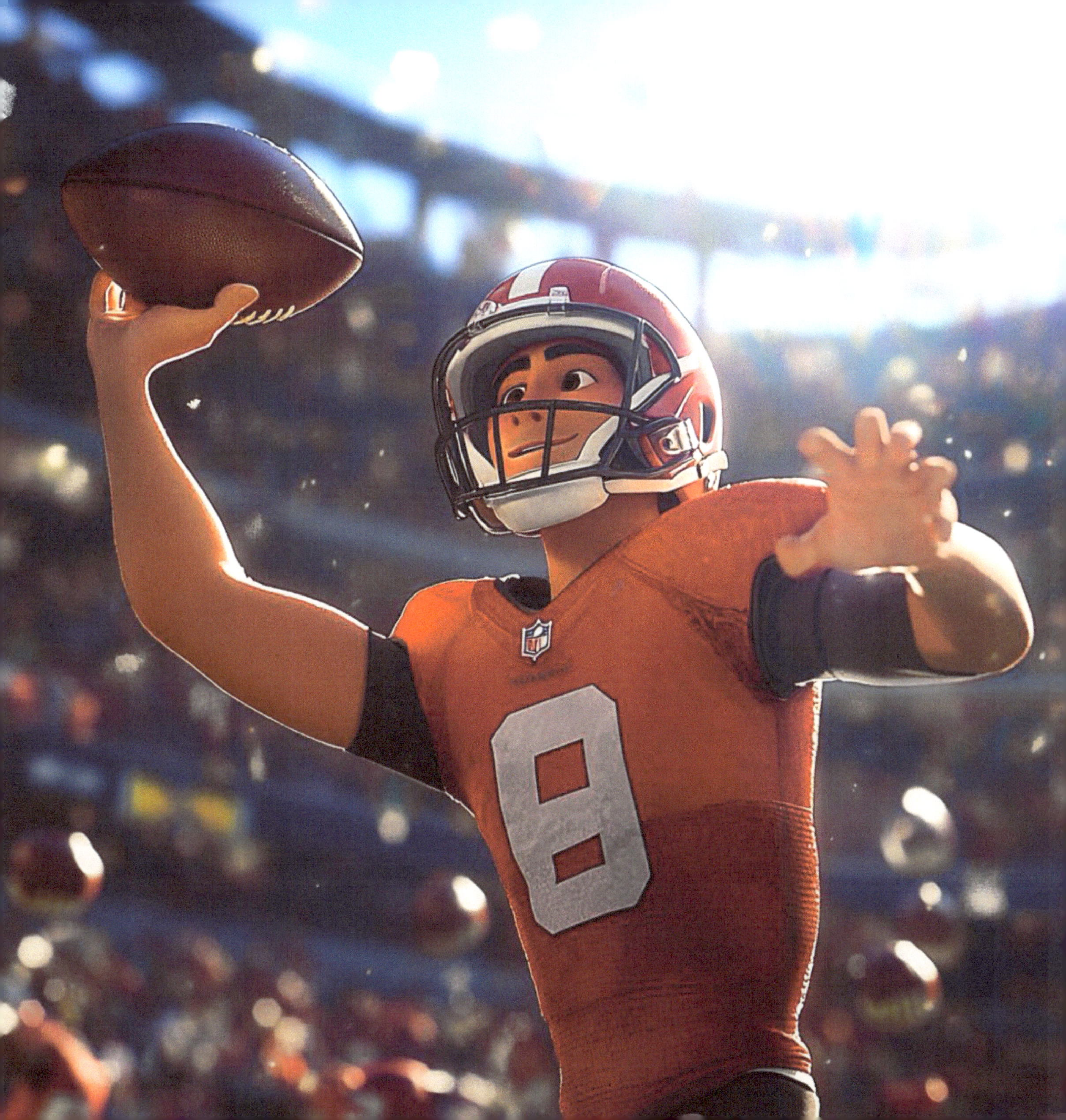

Abby put together a plan to get her fellow townspeople to remember the magic of Thanksgiving.

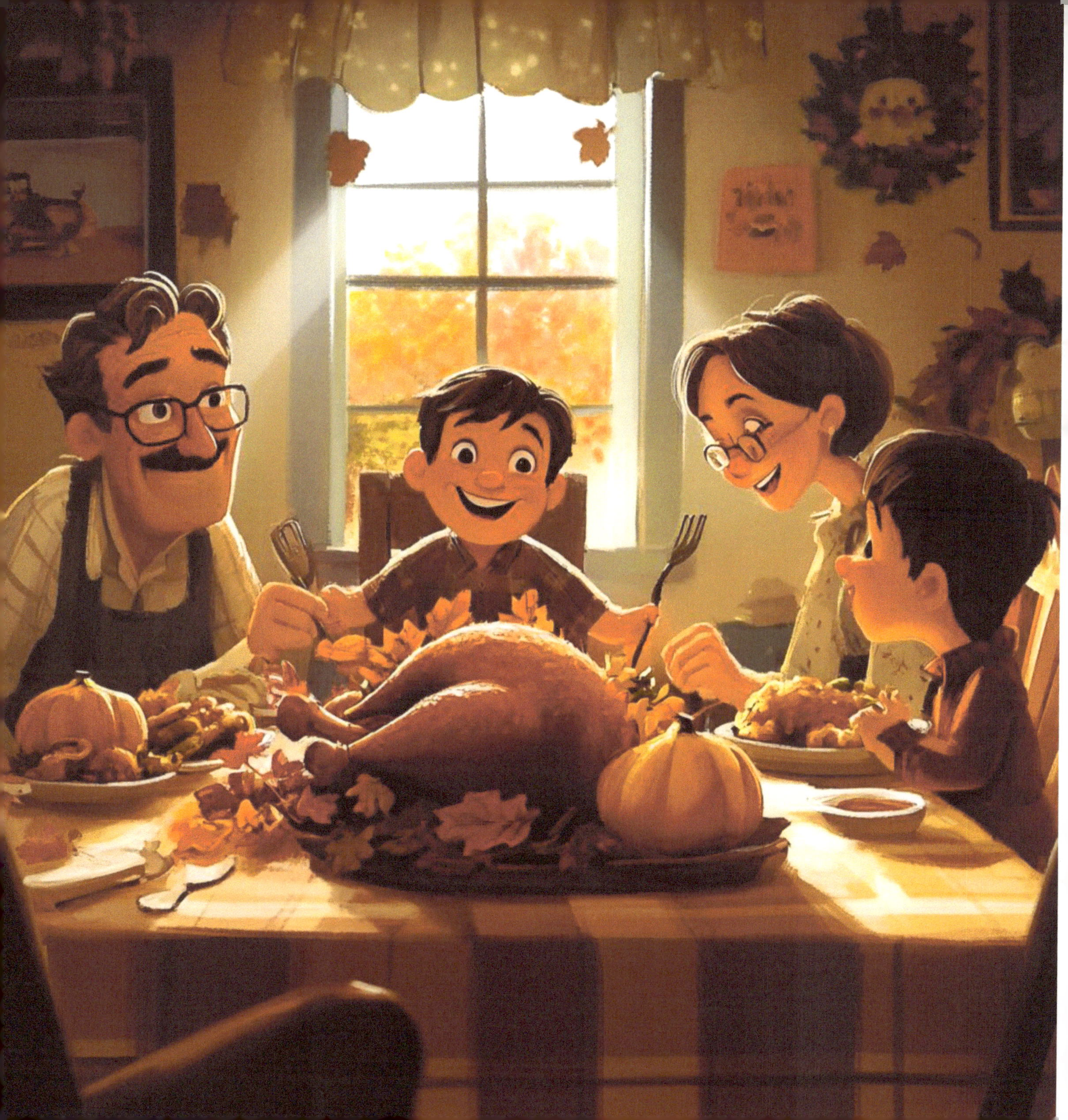

She went to the electronics store to set up a giant projector for the football game. Abby went to the local catering company to provide a Thanksgiving feast.

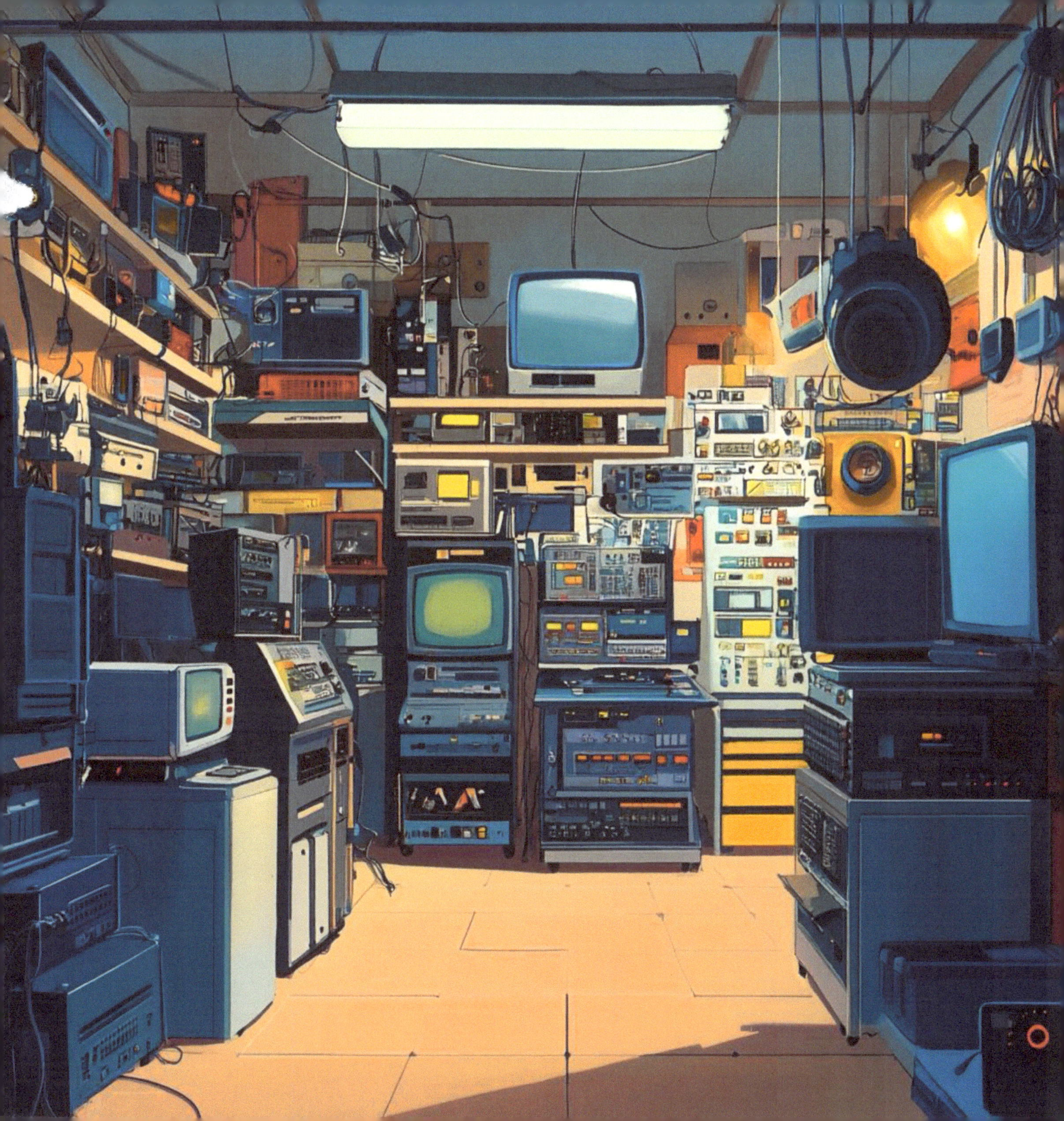

After all the running around,
Abby gathered the townspeople
to enjoy Thanksgiving.
They celebrated and thanked
the girl for reminding
them of the magic of Thanksgiving.

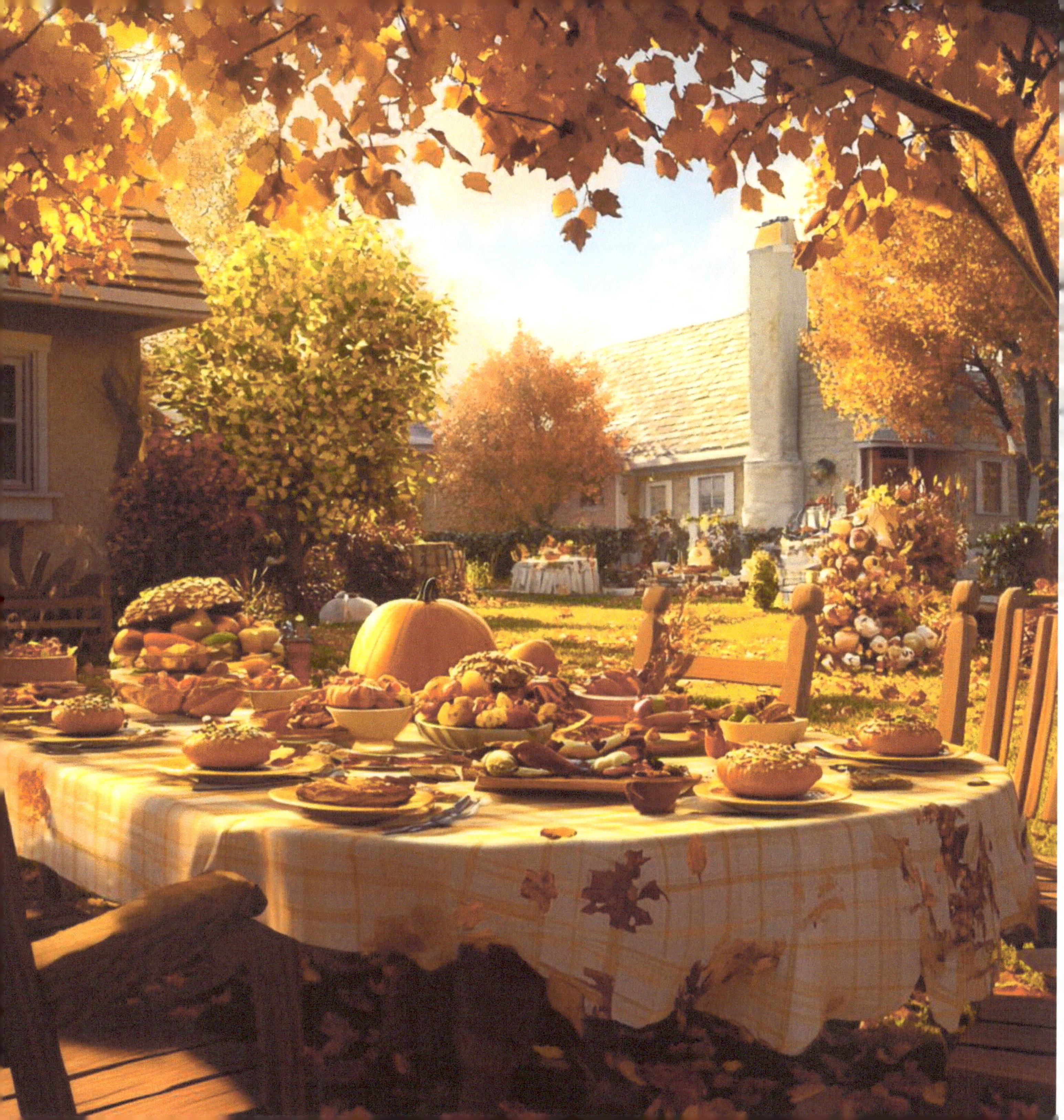

The End

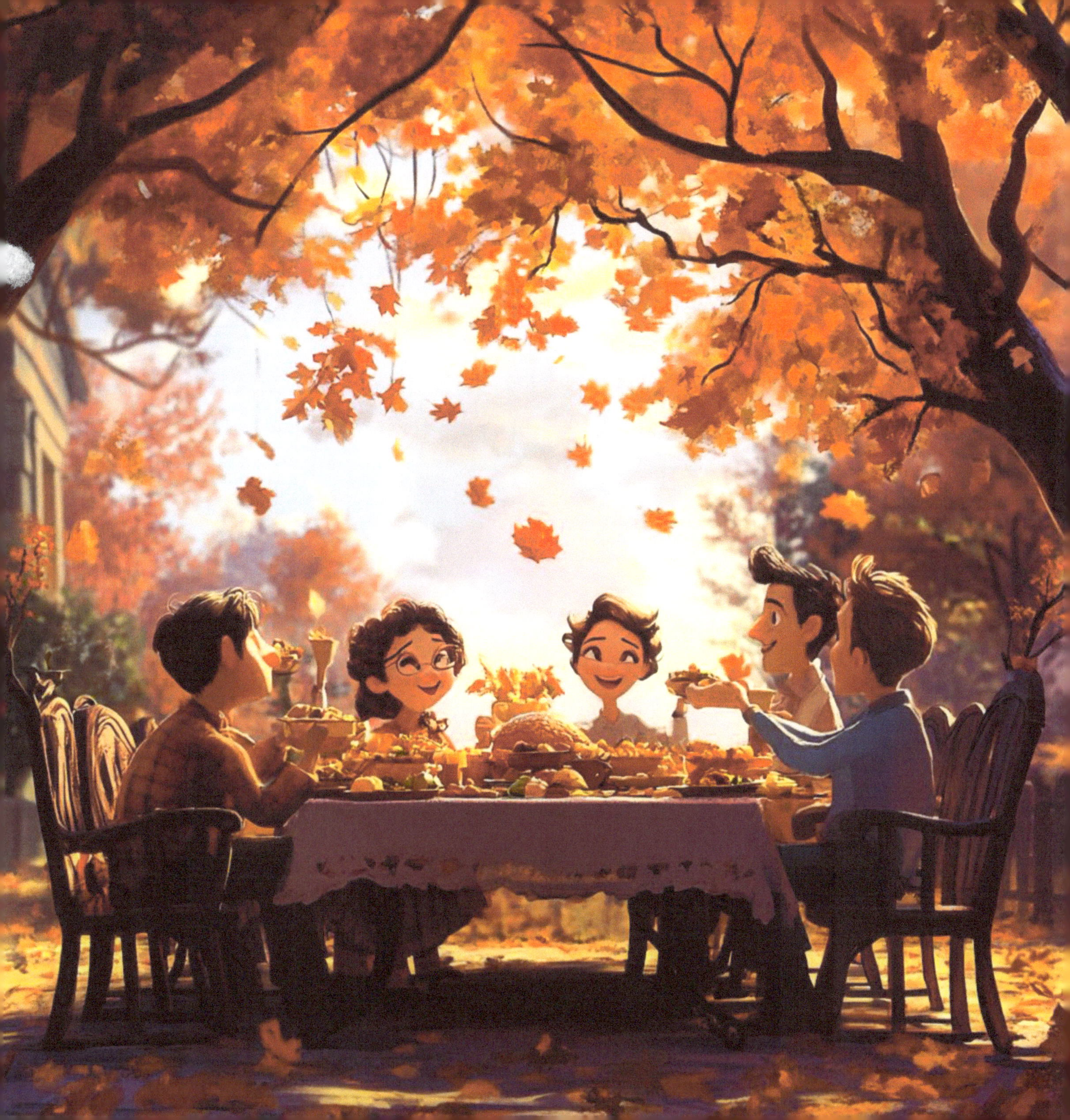

CW01163238

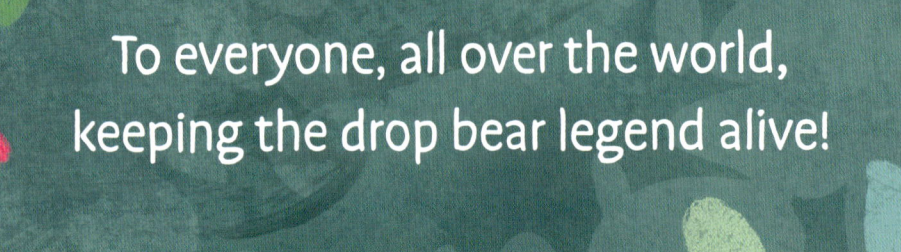

To everyone, all over the world,
keeping the drop bear legend alive!

Scholastic Press
An imprint of Scholastic Australia Pty Limited (ABN 11 000 614 577)
PO Box 579 Gosford NSW 2250
www.scholastic.com.au

Part of the Scholastic Group
Sydney • Auckland • New York • Toronto • London • Mexico City
New Delhi • Hong Kong • Buenos Aires • Puerto Rico

Published by Scholastic Australia in 2022.
Text and illustrations copyright © Heath McKenzie, 2022.

The moral rights of Heath McKenzie have been asserted.

All rights reserved. No part of this publication may be reproduced or transmitted in any form
or by any means, electronic or mechanical, including photocopying, recording, storage in
an information retrieval system, or otherwise, without the prior written permission of the
publisher, unless specifically permitted under the Australian Copyright Act 1968 as amended.

A catalogue record for this
book is available from the
National Library of Australia

ISBN: 978-1-76112-139-5

Typeset in Duper and Arvindh Handsans.

Design by Nicole Stofberg.

Heath McKenzie created these illustrations digitally.

Printed in China by RR Donnelley.
Scholastic Australia's policy, in association with RR Donnelley, is to use papers that
are renewable and made efficiently from wood grown in responsibly managed forests,
so as to minimise its environmental footprint.

10 9 8 7 6 5 4 3 2 1   22 23 24 25 26 / 2

Beware, Beware the Drop Bear!

Heath McKenzie

A Scholastic Press book from Scholastic Australia

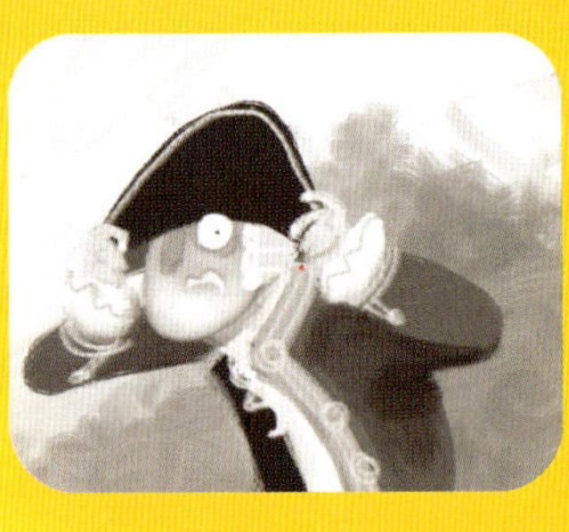
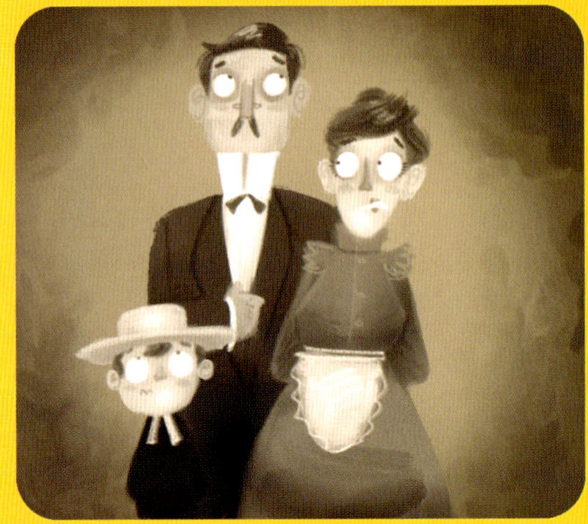
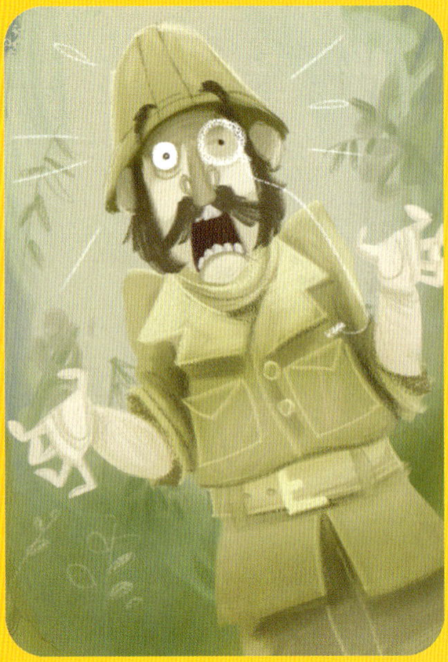
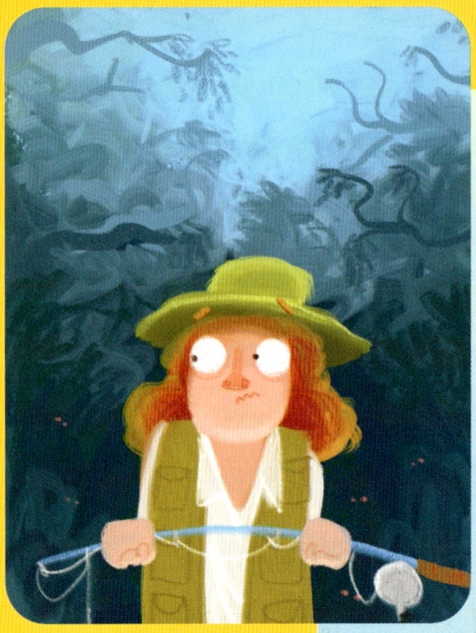
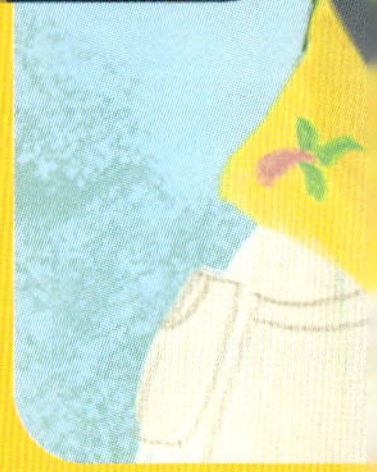
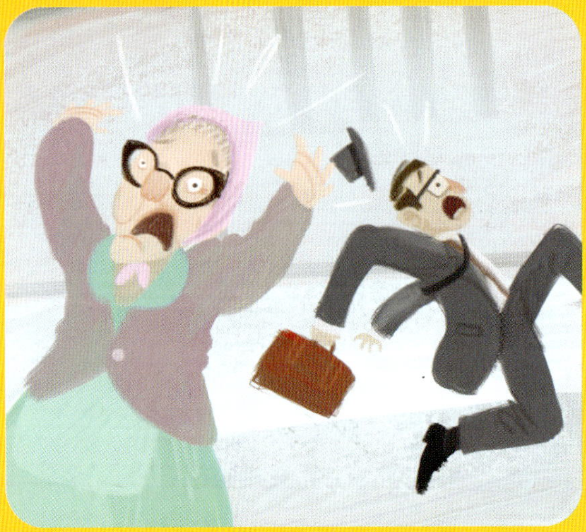
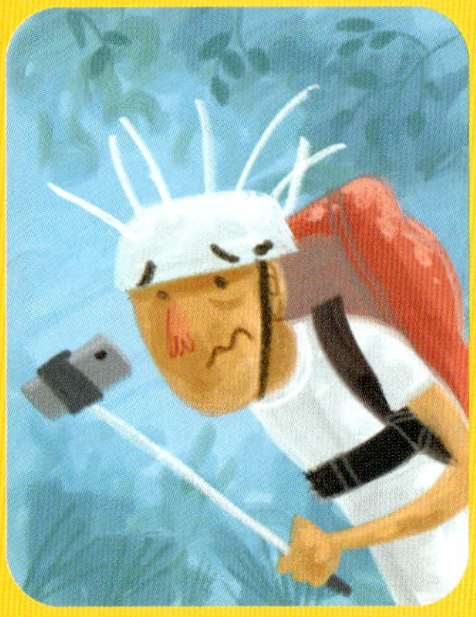
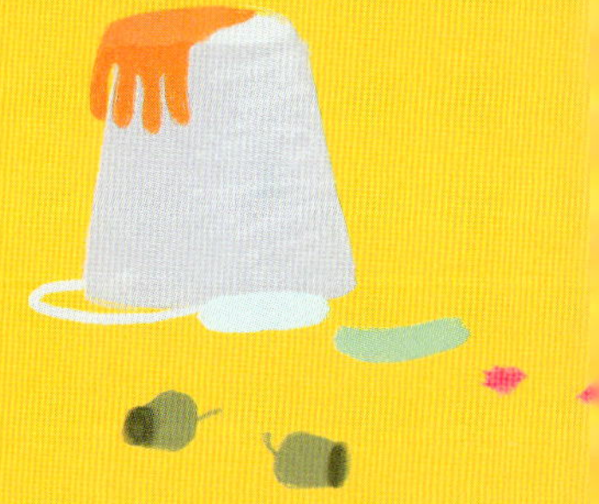

For many **long** years,
tales have been spread,
that fill (mostly tourists)
with **horror** and **dread.**

Tales about **creatures** all covered in hair, that **strike** from above . . .

THE DREADED DROP BEAR!

While Aussies in general
are comfy with **claws**,
and **slithery** scales
and great **gnashing** jaws.

And willing to put up with **fins** in the sea,

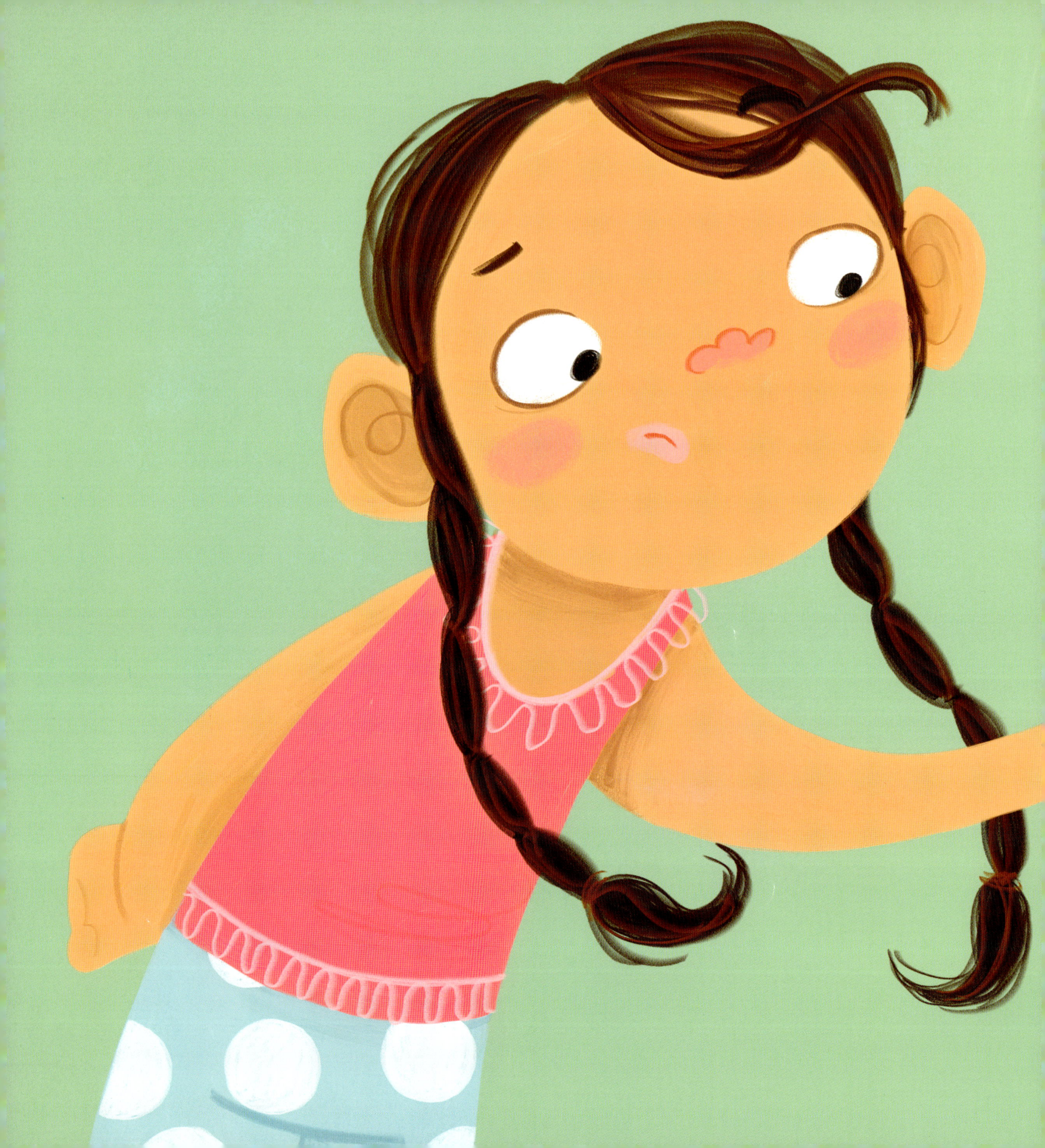

and **eight legs** backstroking in their cups of tea.

When it comes to these **beasts** lurking on high,
well, let's just say they've made the **toughest** kids **cry!**

Apparently, according to the **lucky few**
who claim that they've seen one and survived the view,
these **terrible bears** reside in the branches
and dangle there, silently waiting for chances
to **drop** from above when you pass underneath.

The last thing you'll see is a flash of **sharp teeth!**

They look like **big gumnuts,** and have **beady** eyes,
and cling to the branches with mighty **thick** thighs.

Their arms are quite **bendy,**

their toes rather **long.**

Their **thin ropy** tails end with a **sharp prong!**

They're also quite skinny

and curl like a snake,

and oddly they **smell** just a bit like **cheesecake!**

Their **eyes** are like burning red, fat **jellybeans.**

They say they've a fondness for **stealing** blue jeans!

Also, if you **sing** to them just long enough, they'll give you a **voucher** for discounts on stuff!

And if you can **wrestle** one down from the trees, you'll find you can **squeeze lemonade** from their knees!

20% off SINGING LESSONS

WAIT! WAIT! WAIT!!!

So let me get this straight . . .

These bears that you speak of, that **drop** from the trees,
that look like **big** gumnuts with **lemonade** knees,
with long **dangly** toes on their **hefty** great thighs,
and **burning** red jellybeans stuck on for eyes,

that seem to also be as **skinny** as snakes
with **prongy** rope tails that **whiff** of cheesecake,
whose arms are all **bendy**, the better to **grab ya**,
or maybe to hand you a free discount voucher...

they are actually,
really **REAL?!**

Oh yeah, yeah!

Quite truly, you'd best watch your backs,

and hold on quite tight to those nice denim dacks!

If faint wafts of cheesecake drift by in the air,

you'd better be careful, you'd **better beware!**

You'd better look up
and you'd better **run fast** . . .
for maybe the drop bears
have found you **at LAST!**

HA!
HA!
HA!

Gets 'em every time!

'What's all this **rot** about us being deadly? Why, we're no more scary than a cuddly teddy.'

'Too right, we're as harmless as **harmless** can be . . .

. . . unless we nod off and drop out of a tree!'